# The Poetry of Bliss Carman

## Volume XII - Pipes of Pan No III. Songs of the Sea Children

### Dedicated to James Whitcomb Riley

William Bliss Carman was born in Fredericton, in New Brunswick on April 15th 1861.  He was educated at Fredericton Collegiate School before moving to the University of New Brunswick, obtaining his B.A. there in 1881. As is common with so many writers his first published piece was for the University magazine and for Carman that was in 1879.

After several years editing various magazines and periodicals Carman first published a poetry volume in 1893 with Low Tide on Grand Pré.  There was no Canadian company prepared to publish and when an American company did so it went bankrupt.

The following year was decidedly better.  His partnership with the American poet Richard Hovey had given birth to Songs of Vagabondia. It was an immediate success.

That success prompted the Boston firm, Stone & Kimball, to reissue Low Tide on Grand Pré and to hire Carman as the editor of its literary journal, The Chapbook.

Carman brought out, in 1895, Behind the Arras, a somewhat more serious and philosophical work centered on the premise of a long meditation, using the speaker's house and its many rooms, as a symbol of life and the choices to be made.

In 1896 Carman met Mrs Mary Perry King, who rapidly became patron, adviser and sometime lover. She also became his writing collaborator on two verse dramas.

In 1897 Carman published Ballad of Lost Haven, and in 1898, By the Aurelian Wall, the title poem itself was an elegy to John Keats and the book was a collection of formal elegies.

As the century turned Carman was hard at work on a five-volume set of poetry "Pans Pipes". The excellence of a number of these poems did much to install Carman as the most noted of Canadian Poets and eventually their own Poet Laureate.

In 1912 the final work in the Vagabondia series was published. Richard Hovey had died in 1900 and so this last work was purely Carman's. It has a distinct elegiac tone as if remembering the past works themselves.

On October 28th, 1921 Carman was honored by the newly-formed Canadian Authors' Association where he was crowned Canada's Poet Laureate with a wreath of maple leaves.

William Bliss Carman died of a brain hemorrhage at the age of 68 in New Canaan on the 8th June, 1929.

## Index of Contents

PRELUDE

These are the little songs
The wild sea children sang,
When the first gold arch of light
From rim to zenith sprang;

When all the glad clean joys
Of being came to birth,
Out of the darkling womb
Of the morning of the earth.

And these are the lyric songs
The earthborn children sing,
When wild-wood laughter throngs

The shy bird-throats of spring;

When there's not a joy of the heart
But flies like a flag unfurled,
And the swelling buds bring back
The April of the world.

These are the April songs
The vernal children sing,
When the yellow pollen dust
Floats on the stream in spring;

When the swelling streams go down
Through the deep and grassy floors,
And the gold-fish and the turtle
Bask at their river doors.

And these are the innocent songs
The forest children sing,
When the whippoorwill's unrest
Is a pulse in the heart of spring;

When the dark of the frail new moon
Is a globe of dim sea green,
And no soul fears what its strange
Sea-memories may mean.

These are the happy songs
The first sea children made,
When the red morning roused them
In the deep forest shade;

When Hillborn said to Seaborn,
"Sweetheart, but thou art fair!"
And the shining silver sea-mist
Made moonstones in her hair.

These are the lilting songs
The dark sea children knew,
When the sands emerged, and the sea
Was a lotus of Indian blue;

When, blossom by wind-blown blossom,
Their virginal zones undone,
The world was a wide sunflower
Turning her face to the sun.

SONGS OF THE SEA CHILDREN

I.

There is a wise Magician,
Who sets a yellow star
To seal the cinders of the night
Within a hollow jar.

And when the jar is broken,
A marvel has been done;
There lies within the rosy dusk
That coal we call the sun.

But more than any wonder
That makes the rose of dawn,
Is this inheritance of joy
My heart is happy on.


II.

The day is lost without thee,
The night has not a star.
Thy going is an empty room
Whose door is left ajar.

Depart: it is the footfall
Of twilight on the hills.
Return: and every rood of ground
Breaks into daffodils.

Thy coming is companioned
By presences of bliss;
The rivers and the little leaves
All know how good it is.


III.

Thou art the sense and semblance
Of things that never were,
The meaning of a sunset,
The tenor of a star.

Thou art the trend of morning,
The burden of June's prime,
The twilight's consolation,
The innocence of time.

Thou art the phrase for gladness
God coined when he was young,
The fare-thee-well to sadness
By stars of morning sung,

The lyric revelation
To rally and rebuoy
The darker earth's half sinking
Temerity of joy.

Out of the hush and hearkening
Of the reverberant sea,
Some happier golden April
Might fashion things like thee.

Or if one heart-beat faltered
In oblivion's drum-roll,
That perfect idle moment
Might be thy joyous soul.

And the long waves of sorrow
Will search and find no shore
In all the seas of being,
When thou shalt be no more.


IV.

Thou art the pride and passion
Of the garden where God said,
"Let us make a man." To fashion
The beauty of thy head,

The iron æons waited
And died along the hill,
Nor saw the uncreated
Dream of the urging will.

A thousand summers wandered
Alone beside the sea,
And guessed not, though they pondered,
What his design might be.

But here in the sun's last hour,
(So fair and dear thou art!)
He shuts in my hand his flower,
His secret in my heart.


V.


In the door of the house of life,
Beside the fabled sea,
I am a harpstring in the wind,
Æolian for thee.

It was a cunning idler
Who strung the even cords
Across the drift of harmonies
Impossible to words.

It was the old Musician,
With nothing else to do,
One April when he felt the stir
Revive him and renew,

Made me thy naught but lover,
A frayed imperfect strand
Reverberant to every note,
Alive beneath thy hand!

But smile, and I am laughter;
Look sorrow, and I mourn —
A spirit from the cave of fears,
Fantastic and forlorn.

Sing low — the world is waiting
Such radiance as thine
To welcome her returning ships
Above the dark sea-line.

Rejoice — I know the cadence,
Thou innocent and glad,
To make of every hillside flower
A dancing Oread.

A thing of sense and spirit,
And moods and melody,
I am a harpstring in the wind,

Æolian for thee.

VI.

Love, by that loosened hair,
Well now I know
Where the lost Lilith went
So long ago.

Love, by those starry eyes
I understand
How the sea maidens lure
Mortals from land.

Love, by that welling laugh
Joy claims its own
Sea-born and wind-wayward
Child of the sun.

VII.

Once more in every tree-top
I hear the hollow wind
A-blowing the last remnants
Of winter from the land.

Far down the April morning,
With battle-clang and glee,
The Boreal intruders
Are driven to the sea.

Then softly, buds of scarlet,
Warm rain, and purple wing —
The tattered glad uncumbered
Camp-followers of spring!

VIII.

Under the greening willow
Wanders a golden cry;
Oriole April up in the world
With morning day goes by.

Out of the virgin quiet
Like an awakening sigh,
With the wild, wild heart forever
A journeyer am I.

We are the wind's own brothers,
Sorrow and joy and I;
But thou art the hope of morrows
That shall be by and by.


IX.

Dear, what hast thou to do
With the cold moon,
Free to range, fleet to change,
So far and soon?

Dear, what hast thou to do
With the hoar sea?
Love alone is his own
Eternity.

Dear, what hast thou to do
With anything
In the wide world beside
Joyance and spring?


X.

As sudden winds that freak
The fresh face of the sea,
The tinge upon her cheek
Tells what the storm will be.

As purple shadows rise
Up to the setting sun,
Her wonderful grey eyes
Will tell when love is done.


XI.

As down the purple of the night
I watch the flaring meteors race,
The gorgeous Bedouins of the dusk
Making across the glooms of space,

To my fantastic heart's unrest
That would be gay, that would be gone,
They seem like trysting lovers' souls
Too long delayed and hurrying on.


XII.


In the Kingdom of Boötes,
Whose vast cordon none can tell,
Mirac answers to Arcturus,
"All is well!"

What to them are days and seasons,
Storm and triumph, plague and war —
With their large, serene appointments,
Star for star?

In this handbreadth of the midnight,
These heart-confines where we dwell,
I can hear your spirit answer,
"All is well!"

What to us is night or morrow,
Or the little pause of death,
In the rhythm of joy we measure
Breath by breath?


XIII.


Look, love, along the low hills
The first stars!
God's hand is lighting the watchfires for us,
To last until dawn.

Hark, love, the wild whippoorwills!
Those weird bars,
Full of dark passion, will pierce the dim forest,
All night, on and on,

Till the overbrimmed bowl of life spills,
And time mars
The one perfect piece of his handcraft, love's lifetime
From dewrise till dawn.

Foolish heart, fearful of ills!
Shall the stars
Require a reason, the birds ask a morrow?
Heed thou love alone!


XIV.


The rain-wind from the East,
So long a wanderer
Beyond the sources of the sun,
Brings back the crocus April and the showers.
A heart upwelling in the forest flowers
Has made them lovers every one.
Who makes the twilight seem to stir
In happy tears released?
There, there, sweetheart!

The night-wind from the West,
The broad eaves of the sky,
Brings back across the orchard hills
The memories of a thousand springs with him;
And the white apple valleys in a dream
Listen to the dark whippoorwills.
Is the old burden of their joy
So great they cannot rest?
There, there, sweetheart!


XV.


O purple-black are the wet quince boughs,
Where the buds begin to burn!
And fair enough is Spring's new house,
Made fresh for Love's return.

She has taken him in and locked the door,
And thrown away the key.
When Free-foot finds his Rove-no-more,
What use is liberty?

XVI.

An unseen hand went over the hill,
And lit the cresset stars,
And below the summer sea was strewn
With mysterious nenuphars.

The little wind of twilight came
With the gladdest of words to me,
"The tide is full, the night is fair,
And Her window waits for thee!"


XVII.

The very sails are singing
A song not of the wind;
A fire dance is creaming
Our wake that runs behind.

In all the shining splendid
White moonflower of the sea,
There's not a runnel sleeping
For ecstasy of thee.


XVIII.

Where the blue comes down to the brine,
And the brine goes up to the blue,
It's shine, shine, shine,
The whole day through,
The whole summer day long, dear.

Till the sun like a harbour buoy,
Is riding afloat in the west,
And it's joy, joy, joy,
For the place of his rest,
The haven of No-more-fear.

Then the stars come out on the sea,
To dance on the purple floor.
Their Master has turned the key
In the silver door,

And my heart's delight draws near.

As if the sea's eternal rote
Might cease to set remembrance wild,
The breezy hair, the lyric throat
Were given to the surf-born child.

And the great forest found a voice
For her along the brookside brown,
That bids the purple dusk rejoice,
And croons the golden daylight down.

O wind and stars, I am with you now;
And ports of day, Good-by!
When my captain Love puts out to sea,
His mariner am I.

I set my shoulder to the prow,
And launch from the pebbly shore.
The tide pulls out, and hints of time
Blow in from the cool sea floor.

My sheering sail is a swift white wing
Crowding the gloom with haste;
I scud through the large and solemn world,
And skim the wan grey waste.

O stars and wind, be with me now;
And ports of night, draw near!
No sooner the longed for seamark shines,
Than the very dark grows dear.

All the zest of all the ages
Shimmers in my sea-bird's wing,
Flickering above the surges
Of the sea.

All the quiet of the ages
Slumbers in my sea-bird's wing,
Where it settles down the verges
Of the sea.

All the questing soul's behesting
Pent and freed in one white wing,
Joying there above the dirges
Of the sea.

Be thou, sweetheart, such a sweetheart!
All the valour of the spring
Crowds thy pulses with the urges
Of the sea;

Till this drench of joy, thou sweetheart,
Fills the spaces of the spring,
And the large fresh night emerges
From the sea.


XXII.

Eyes like the blue-green
Shine of the sea,
Where the swift shadows run,
Whose soul is free.

Shimmer of sunlight,
Shadow of gloom,
Wayward as ecstasy,
Solemn as doom.

Triumph, transplendour,
Joy through and through,
Till the soul wonders what
Sense next may do.

Hair like the blown grass
Brown on the hill,
Where the wide wandering
Wind has his will.

Spirit, the nomad,
Whither to wend,
Knows not and fears not,

To the world's end.

Seadusk or Dawnbright
Name the earth's child,
Like the wind, like the sea,
Virginal wild.


XXIII.


"Crimson bud, crimson bud,
How come you here,
Daring the upper world,
Blithe without fear?"

"Goldy plume, goldy plume,
Ages ago,
Came to my House of Dark
One through the snow."

"Crimson bud, crimson bud,
What was the word,
Down in the frozen earth,
Sleeping, you heard?"

"Goldy plume, goldy plume,
Deep in the mould,
Somebody whispered me,
'Budkin, be bold!'"

"Crimson bud, crimson bud,
What was his name —
Taught you such valour
And girt you with flame?"

"Ah, fellow wayfarer,"
Whispered the gloom,
"When they shall question, say,
Love bade me come!"


XXIV.


We wandered through the soft spring days,
And heard the flowers
Talking among themselves of joys

That were not ours.

Till April in a softening mood
Faltered a word
The pretty gossips of the wood
Had scarcely heard.

But somehow you, you caught the lilt
Of that wild speech
The tiny tribesmen found occult
Beyond their reach.

Now when the rainman walks the field,
And robin sings,
I hark to promises that hold
A thousand springs.


XXV.

You pipers in the swales,
Tune up your reedy flutes,
And blow and blow to bring me back
My little girl in spring!

Take all the world beside,
And flute it far away
For less than nought, but give me back
One sleepless night in spring.


XXVI.

To-night I hear the rainbirds
Piercing the silver gloom;
The scent of the sea-blown lilacs
Wanders across my room.

Caught in their wake I follow
The drift of memory;
Once more the summer twilight
Settles upon the sea.

I shut my eyes and see you
Under the lilacs stand,
While the soft mists of sea-rain

Are blowing in to land.

Your little hands steal upward,
Our fingers interlace;
And through the driving sea-dark
I feel your burning face.

One little hour of heaven
Lost in a single kiss;
And then we two forever
The castaways of bliss.

To-night the scent of lilacs
Comes up to me again,
And ghosts of buried summers
Walk with the lonely rain.

But ah, what rooftree shelters
To-night the dear black head?
Only the sea wind answers —
And leaves of the word unsaid.


XXVII.

Lord of the vasty tent of heaven,
Who hast to thy saints and sages given
A thousand nights with their thousand stars,
And the star of faith for a thousand years,

Grant me, only a foolish rover
All thy beautiful wide world over,
A thousand loves in a thousand days,
And one great love for a thousand years.


XXVIII.

In the cool of dawn I rose;
Life lay there from hill to hill
In the core of a blue pearl,
As it seemed, so deep and still.

Not a word the mountains said
Of the day that was to be,
As I crossed them, till you came

At the sunrise back with me.

Then we heard the whitethroat sing,
And the world was left behind.
A new paradise arose
Out of his untarnished mind.

The brown road lay through the wood,
And the forest floor was spread
For our footing with the fern,
And the cornel berries red.

There the woodland rivers sang;
Not a sorrow touched their glee,
Dancing up the yellow sun,
From the purple mountain sea.

Towns and turbulence and fame
Were as fabled things that lay
Through the gateway of the notch,
Long ago and far away.

There we loitered and went on,
Where the roadside berries grew;
Earth with all its joy once more
Was made over for us two.

And at last a meaning filled
The round morning fair and good,
Waited for a thousand years,
There was no more solitude.


XXIX.

Up from the kindled pines,
Lo, the lord Sun!
What shall his children find
When day is done?

Ere thy feet follow him
Over the sea,
Love, turn thy glorious
Eyes once to me!

High in the burning noon,
Lo, the lord Sun

Sleeps, with his hand slack,
His girdle undone.

Ere thy feet follow him
Over the hill,
Love, lace thy heart to mine,
Time has stood still.

Down by the valley-night
Sings the great sea;
Over the mountain rim
Day walks for thee.

Ere thy feet follow him
Into far lands,
Love, lift thy mouth to me
Up through thy hands!

Well do they journey
Who joy as they go;
Hear his hills whispering,
"So, it is so."

Ere thy feet follow him
Down to the shade,
Love, loose thy zone to me,
Mistress and maid!

Down to the kindling pines,
Lo, the lord Sun
Goes unreluctant
And day is done.


XXX.

The skiey shreds of rain
Are all blown loose again,
And bright among the dripping chestnut boles
Whistle the orioles.

As if wise Nature knew
The finest thing to do,
And touched her forestry, supremely done,
With these few flakes of sun.

To-night by the June sea

You are come hack to me,
Through all the mellow dark from hill to hill
That gladdens and grows still;

As though wise Nature guessed
Her love joys were the best,
When down the darkling spaces of desire
She sent your song and fire.

## XXXI.

On the meridian of the night
Alcar the Tester marks high June;
Arcturus knows his zenith fame;
No grass-head sleeps upon the dune.

And up from the southeastern sea,
Antares, the red summer star,
Brings back the ardours of the earth,
Like fire opals in a jar:

The frail and misty sense of things
Beyond mortality's ado,
The soft delirium of dream,
And joy pale virgins never knew.

## XXXII.

Love, lift your longing face up through the rain!
In the white drench of it over the hills,
Blurring remembrance and quieting pain,
Stretch the strong hands of the sea.

Love, lift your longing face up through the rain!
In the bleak rote of it through the far hills,
Rhythmed to joy and untarnished of pain,
Calls the great heart of the sea.

## XXXIII.

Swing down, great sun, swing down,
And beat at the gates of day,

To open and let thee forth!
I would not have thee stay.

Swing up, dear stars, and shine
Over the baths of the sea!
To-night, my beautiful one
Will open her arms for me.


XXXIV.

The world is a golden calyx,
A-swing in the blooth of time,
Where floret to floret ripens
And the starry blossoms rhyme.

Thou art the fair seed vessel
Waiting all day for me,
Who ache with the golden pollen
The night will spill for thee.


XXXV.

Eyes like summer after sundown,
Hands like roses after dew,
Lyric as a blown rose garden
The wind wanders through.

Swelling breasts that bud to crimson,
Hair like cobwebs after dawn,
And the rosy mouth wind-rifled
When the wind is gone.


XXXVI.

The sun is lord of a manor fair,
And the earth his garden old,
Whose dewy beds where he walks at morn
Flower by flower unfold.

When he goes at night and leaves the stars
Lit in the trees to shine,
Blossom by blossom the flowerheads sleep —

And a rosy head by mine.


XXXVII.

In God's blue garden the flowers are cold,
As you tell them over star by star,
Sirius, Algol, pale Altair,
Lone Arcturus, and Algebar.

In love's red garden the flowers are warm,
As I count them over and kiss them by,
From the sultry royal rose-red mouth
To the last carnation dusk and shy.


XXXVIII.

First by her starry gaze that falls
Aside, as if afraid to know
The stronger self who stirs and calls,
I think she came from a land of snow.

Then by her mood that melts to mine
Her body and her soul's desire,
Under the shifting forest shine,
I think she came from a land of fire.


XXXIX.

The alchemist who throws his worlds
In the round crucible of the sun,
Has laid our bodies in the forge
Of love to weld them into one.

The hypnotist who waves his hand
And the pale streamers walk the night,
A moment for our souls unbars
The lost dominions of delight.


XL.

Thy mouth is a snow apple,
Thy tongue a rosy melon core,
Thy breasts are citrons odorous of the East.
I know that nursery tale of Eden now,
Where God prepared the feast
Beneath the bow.
I ask no more.

The apple-trees have whispered
The only word I listened for
Through all the legends babbled in my ears.
I know what manner of unbitten fruit
The first man took with fears
And found so sweet.
I ask no more.

XLI.

As orchards in an apple land,
That whiten to the moon of May,
Hear the first rainbird's ecstasy
Peal from the dark hills far away;

The wintry spaces of my soul,
Snowed under by the drift of time,
Feel immortality begin
As your long kisses surge and climb.

XLII.

Noon on the marshes and noon on the hills,
And joy in the white sail that shivers and fills.

Gold are the grain lands, and gold is the sea,
And gold is my little love maid to me.

XLIII.

Berrybrown, Berrybrown, give me your hands!
Here in the bracken shade will we not well
Wring the warm summer world dry of its honey?
God made a heaven before He made hell.

Berrybrown, Berrybrown, give me your eyes;
Let their shy quivering rapture and deep
Melt as they merge in mine melting above them!
God made surrender before He made sleep.

Berrybrown, Berrybrown, give me your mouth,
Till all is done 'twixt a breath and a breath!
Naught shall undo the one joy-deed for ever,
God made desire before He made death.


XLIV.

Wait for me, Cherrychild, when the blue dusk
Falls from the silent star-spaces and fills
With utter peace the great heart of the hills,
Child, Cherrychild!

Call to me, Cherrychild, when the blue dusk
First throbs to passion among the dark hills,
In the brown throats of the lone whippoorwills,
Child, Cherrychild!

Come to me, Cherrychild, in the blue dusk!
Forlorn and loverless as the wild sea,
Long have I lain alone, longing for thee,
Child, Cherrychild.


XLV.

Summer love, open your eyes to me now!
June's on the mountain and day's at the door.
Time shall turn back for us one crimson hour,
Ere the white seraph winds walk the sea floor.

Summer heart, open your arms to me now!
Beautiful wonder-eyed spirit's home, here
With the eternal ache quenched in the bliss,
One golden minute outmeasures a year.

Sweet heaven! Open your arms to me now!
There, dearest body, cease trembling, lie still!
Joy, how the June birds are shivered with song!
And see, the first shreds of dawn over the hill.

Through what strange garden ran
The sultry stream whereon
This languorous nenuphar of love could grow?
Such melting ardours spending to the moon,
From swoon to swoon!

My wondrous moonflower white,
Outspread in the warm night,
Tinged with a rosy tint, a golden glow,
And fervours of enchantment it must hide
Till daylight died.

It lies so soft and fond,
Wilted in my hot hand,
That was so dewy fresh an hour ago.
"Can life be, then," my soul is pondering,
"So frail a thing?"

And all because I laid
The snowy petals wide;
Having heard tell, yet longing still to know,
What sweet things youth might barter ignorance for,
Once and no more.


XLVII.

Let the red dawn surmise
What we shall do,
When this blue starlight dies
And all is through.

If we have loved but well
Under the sun,
Let the last morrow tell
What we have done.


XLVIII.

A breath upon my face,

A whisper at my ear,
Filling this leafy place,
Tell me love is here.

The sea-gloom of her eyes,
The apples of her breast,
The shadows where she lies,
A-tremble or at rest,

The little rosy knees,
The beech-brown of her hair —
A thousand things like these
Tell me love is fair.

The clinging of her kiss,
Her heart that looks beyond,
The joys she will not miss,
Tell me love is fond.

And when I am away,
A weary dying fall,
Haunting the wind by day,
Tells me love is all.


XLIX.

I was a reed in the stilly stream,
Heigh-ho!

And thou my fellow of moveless dream,
Heigh-lo.

Hardly a word the river said,
As there we bowed him a listless head:

Only the yellowbird pierced the noon;
And summer died to a drowsier swoon,

Till the little wind of night came by,
With the little stars in the lonely sky,

And the little leaves that only stir,
When shiest wood-fellows confer.

It shook the stars in their purple sphere,
And laid a frost on the lips of fear.

It woke our slumbering desire,
As a breath that blows a mellow fire,

And the thrill that made the forest start,
Was a little sigh from our happy heart.

This is the story of the world,
Heigh-ho!
This is the glory of the world,
Heigh-lo.


L.

I was the west wind over the garden,
Out of the twilit marge and deep;
You were the sultry languorous flower,
Famished and filled and laid to sleep.

I was the rover bee, and you —
With the hot red mouth where a soul might drown,
And the buoyant soul where a man might swim —
You were the blossom that drew me down.


LI.

A touch of your hair, and my heart was furled;
A drift of fragrance, and noon stood still;
All of a sudden the fountain there
Had something to whisper the sun on the hill.

Rose of the garden of God's desire,
Only the passionate years can prove
With sorrow and rapture and toil and tears
The right of the soul to the kingdom of love.


LII.

In the land of kisses
The very winds were stirred
To mortal speech. But this is
The only tale I heard.

In the land of kisses
Your mouth is a red bloom,
Aching to know the blisses
That perish and consume.

In the land of kisses
My mouth is a red moth
Searching in the dusk. And this is
The rapture for us both.


LIII.

I think the sun when he turns at night,
And lays his face against the sea's,
Must have such thoughts as these.

I think the wind, when he wakes at dawn,
Must wonder, seeing hill by hill,
That they can sleep so still.


LIV.

I see the golden hunter go,
With his hound star close at heel,
Through purple fallows above the hill,
When the large autumn night is still
And the tide of the world is low.

And while to their unwearied quest
The sister Pleiads pass,
That seventh loveliest and lost
Desire of all the orient host
Is here upon my breast.


LV.

You old men with frosty beards,
I am wiser than you all;
I have seen a fairer page
Than Belshazzar's wall.

You young men with scornful lips,
I am stronger than you all;
I have sown the Cadmian field
Where no shadows fall.

For a woman yesterday
Loved me, body, soul, and all.
Saints will lift their crowns to me
At the Judgment Call.


LVI.

It was the tranquil hour
Of earth's expectancy,
When we lay on the Wishing Sands
Beside the sleeping sea.

We saw the scarlet moon rise
And light the pale grey land;
We heard the whisper of the tide,
The sighing of the sand.

I felt the ardent flutter
Your heart gave for delight;
You knew how earth is glad and hushed
Under the tent of night.

We dreamed the dream of lovers,
And told our dream to none;
And all that we desired came true,
Because we wished as one.


LVII.

The mountain ways one summer
Saw joy and life go past,
When we who fared so lonely
Were hand in hand at last.

Till over us the pine woods
Their purple shadows cast,
And the tall twilight laid us
Hot mouth to mouth at last.

O hills, beneath your slumber,
Or pines, below your blast,
Make room for your two children,
Cold cheek to cheek at last!


LVIII.

Poppy, you shall live forever
With the crimson of her kiss,
Through a summer day undreamed of
In a land like this.

Once I battered with Oblivion:
For the crimson of her kiss
I would give a thousand morrows
Of a day like this.

But I was a foolish buyer;
For the crimson of her kiss
Woke me, and I heard the wind say,
"Nevermore like this!"

Poppy, you shall sleep forever
With the crimson of her kiss
Through the centuries, undreamed of
In a rhyme like this.


LIX.

I loved you when the tide of prayer
Swept over you, and kneeling there
In the pale summer of the stars,
You laid your cheek to mine.

I loved you when the auroral fire,
Like the world's veriest desire,
Burned up, and as it touched the sea,
You laid your limbs to mine.

I loved you when you stood tiptoe
To say farewell, and let me go
Into the night from your laced arms,
And laid your mouth to mine.

And I shall love you on that day
The wind comes over the sea to say
Your golden name upon men's mouths,
And mix your dust with mine.


LX.


Once of a Northern midnight,
By dike and mountainside,
With fleeces for her habit,
The moon went forth to ride

Up from the ocean caverns,
Where ancient memories bide,
Returning with his secret
We heard the muttering tide.

But fear was not upon you;
Your woman's arms were wide;
The world's poor shreds and tatters
Of mumming laid aside.

The sea-rote for our rubic,
Our ritual and guide,
There was a virgin wedding
Whose vows no priest supplied.

And there until the dawn-wind
Up from the marshes sighed,
Whispered among the aspens,
Shivered and passed and died,

Our scene-shifter the moonlight,
Our orchestra the tide,
I was a prince of fairy,
You were a prince's bride.


LXI.


The forest leaves were all asleep,
The yellow stars were on the hill,
The roving winds were all away,
Only the tide was restless still,

When I awoke. My chamber dim
Was flooded by the cool, sweet night,
And in the hush I seemed aware
Of premonitions of delight.

Who called me lightly as I slept?
Who touched my forehead with soft hands?
Who summoned me without a sound
Back from the vague, mysterious lands?

It must have been my sleepless heart
Knocking upon his prison door,
To bid old Reason have a care
Lest Joy should pass and come no more.


LXII.

There sighed along the garden path
And through the open door a stir;
'Twas not the rustle of the corn,
Nor yet the whisper of the fir.

There passed an Eastern odour, fraught
With the delirium of sense;
'Twas not the attar of the rose,
Nor the carnation's redolence.

Then came a glimmering of white —
The drench of sheer diaphanous lawn,
More palpable than light of stars,
And more delectable than dawn.

The Paphian curve from throat to waist,
From waist to knee, then lost again,
Told me how beauty such as hers
Spreads like a madness among men.


LXIII.

And then I knew the first vague bliss
That swept through Lilith like strange fire,
Consuming all her loveliness
With one imperious desire,

When in the twilight she beheld,
Through the green apple shades obscure,
The Lord God moulding from the dust
Her splendid virgin paramour.

I knew what aching shudder ran
Through the dark bearers, file on file,
When Pharaoh's daughter went to merge
Her peerless beauty in the Nile;

What slumbering deliciousness
Awoke beside the Dorian stream
When the young prince from over sea
Broke on the lovely Spartan's dream;

And all the fervour and desire,
The raptures and the ecstasies,
Of Aucassin and Nicollette,
Of Abelard and Héloïse,

And all the passionate despair,
So bravely borne for many a year,
Of Tristram and the dark Iseult,
Of Launcelot and Guinevere!


LXIV.

I knew, by that diviner sense
Which wakes to beauty sweet and lone,
Once more beneath the moonlit boughs
Astarte had unloosed her zone;

Immortal passion, fair and wild,
Remembering her joys of yore,
Had taken on the human guise
To glad one mortal lover more.


LXV.

A moon-white moth against the moon,
A sea-blue raindrop in the sea,
A grain of pollen on the air,
This little virgin soul might be.

As if a passing breath of wind
Should stir the poplars in the night,
Her wondrous spirit woke from sleep,
And shivered with unknown delight,

As if a sudden garden door
Should open in a granite wall,
She trembled at the brink of joy,
So great and so ephemeral.


LXVI.


What is it to remember?
How white the moonlight poured into the room,
That summer long ago!
How still it was
In that great solemn midnight of the North,
A century ago!

And how I wakened trembling
At soft love-whispers warm against my cheek,
And laughed it was no dream!
Then far away,
The troubled, refluent murmur of the sea,
A sigh within a dream!


LXVII.


She had the fluttering eyelids
Like petals of a rose;
I had the wisdom never learned
From any musty prose.

She had the melting ardour
That hesitates yet dares;
And I had youthful valour's look,
That is so like despair's.

She had the tender bearing
Of daffodils in spring;
And I had sense enough to know
Love is a fleeting thing.

She had the heart of tinder;

I had the lips of flame;
And neither of us ever heard
Procrastination's name.

She had the soft demeanour,
Discreet as any nun's;
And each of us has all the joy
God gives his foolish ones.


LXVIII.

The land lies full, from brim to brim
Of the great smoke-blue mountains' rim,
Of yellow autumn and red sun.
A giant in content, the day
Idles the solemn hours away
To dreamland one by one.

Life is the dominance of good,
And love the ecstasy of mood,
Your hand in my hand says to me.
Yet, somewhere in the waste between
Being and sense, I hear a threne
Wash like the dirging sea.


LXIX.

In the blue opal of a winter noon,
When all the world was a white floor
Lit by the northern sun,
I saw with naked eyes a midday star
Burn on like gleaming spar,
Where all its fellows of the mighty dusk
Had perished one by one.

When I shall have put by the vagrant will,
And down this rover's twilight road
Emerge into the sun,
Be thou my only sheer and single star,
Known, named, and followed far,
When all these Jack-o'-lantern hopes and fears
Have perished one by one!

LXX.

Far hence in the infinite silence
How we shall learn and forget,
Know and be known, and remember
Only the name of regret?

Sown in that ample quiet,
We shall break sheath and climb,
Seeds of a single desire
In the heart of the apple of time.

We shall grow wise as the flowers,
And know what the bluebirds sing,
When the hands of the grasses unravel
The wind in the hollows of spring.

And out of the breathless summer
The aspen leaves will stir,
At your low sweet laugh to remember
The imperfect things we were.


LXXI.

Of the whole year, I think, I love
The best that time we used to call
The Little Summer of All Saints,
About the middle of the fall,

Because there fell the golden days
Of that gold year beside the sea,
When first I had you at heart's will,
And you had your whole will of me.

It is the being's afternoon,
The second summer of the soul,
When spirits find a way to reach
Beyond the sense and its control.

Then come the firmamental days,
The underseason of the year,
When God himself, being well content,
Takes time to whisper in our ear.

Sweetheart, once more by every sign

Of blade and shadow, it must be
The Little Summer of All Saints
In the red Autumn by the sea.


LXXII.

At night upon the mountains
The magic moon goes by,
And stops at every threshold
With lure and mystery.

And then my lonely fancy
Can bide content no more,
But through an autumn country
Must search from door to door,

Till in a quiet valley,
Under a quiet sky,
Is found the one companion
To bid the world good-by.

And once again at moonrise
We wander hand in hand,
With the last grief forgotten,
Through an enchanted land.


LXXIII.

Once more the woods grow crimson,
Once more the year burns down,
Once more my feet come home
To the little seaboard town.

Once more I learn desire
Prevails but to endure,
And the heart springs to meet
Your hand-touch — and be sure.


LXXIV.

Once when the winds of spring came home
From the far countries where they roam,

I heard them tell
Of things I could not understand,
And strange adventures in a land
Where all was well.

I do not wonder any more
What Autumn at his open door
Is dreaming of;
I am so happy to have done
With all the things underneath the sun
Save only love.


LXXV.

The world is swimming in the light,
Sheer as a bubble green and gold.
On the purpureal autumn walls
Once more time's rubric is unrolled.

As if the voice of the blue sea
Sufficed for summer's utmost speech,
But now the very hills must help
And lift their heart to the lyric reach.

Scarlet, diaphanous and glad,
The valiant message waves and burns,
The elemental cry that lurks
Deep as the cold heart of the Norns.


LXXVI.

When the October wind stole in
To wake me in my chamber cool,
With dancing sunlight on the wall,
From the still vestibule

Fluttered a sound like rustling leaves,
Or the just-heard departing stir
Of silk, a hint of presence gone,
A waft of lavender.

I saw upon my arms strange marks,
Traced when my eyes were unaware,
Like petal-stains of some green rose

Or faint kiss-bruises there;

And wondered, as there came the sad
Eternal whisper of the sea,
Which one of all my pale dead loves
Had spent the night with me.


LXXVII.

The red frost came with his armies
And camped by the sides of the sea.
The maples and the oaks took on
His gorgeous livery.

They dyed their tents a madder,
Alizarin and brown,
And dipped their banners in the sun
To give their joy renown.

And lo, when twilight sobered
Their dauntless cinnabars,
Along the outposts of the sea
The watch-fires of the stars!

And I for love of roving
Am listed with the king,
Because I knew the password,
"Joy is the only thing!"


LXXVIII.

Dearest, in this so golden fall,
When beauty aches with her own bliss,
One thought the pause to my desire
And my small consolation is.

I am a child. A thistle seed
On the boon wind is more than I,
Yet will the hand that sows the hills
Have care of me too when I die.

When I who love thee without words
Sink as a foam-bell in the sea,
One who has no regard for fame

Will neither have contempt for me.

Her hair was crocus yellow,
Her eyes were crocus blue,
Her body was the only gate
Of paradise I knew.

Her hands were velvet raptures,
Her mouth a velvet bliss;
Not Lilith in the garden had
So wonderful a kiss.

To know her was to banish
Reason for once and all.
Her voice was like a silver door
Set in a scarlet wall.

For when she said, "I love you,"
It was as when the tide
Yearns for the naked moonlight,
An unreluctant bride.

And when she said, "Ah, leave me,"
It was as when the sea
Sighs at the ebb, or a spent wind
Dies in the aspen tree.

Out of the dust that bore thee,
What wonder walking came, —
What beauty like blown grasses,
What ardour like still flame!

What patience of the mountains,
What yearning of the sea,
What far eternal impulse
Endowed the world with thee?

A reed within the river,
A leaf upon the bough,
What breath of April ever

Was half so dear as thou?


LXXXI.

Remnants of this soul of mine,
This same self that once was me,
Flock and gather and grow one,
Whole once more at thought of thee.

Never yet was such a love,
So supremely fond as thou;
Never mortal lover yet
So beloved as thine is now.

I a foam-head in the sea,
Thou the tide to lift and run;
I a sombre-crested hill,
Thou the purple light thereon.

Tide may ebb and light may fail,
But not love's sincerity, —
More enduring than the sun,
More compelling than the sea.


LXXXII.

What is this House at the End of the World,
Where the sun leaves off and the snow begins,
And the drift of the grey sea spins?

O this is the house where I was born,
At the world's far edge one April day,
Within sound of the white sea spray.

The place is lone, where the hills recede,
And the sea slopes over the world's far side
And nothing moves but the tide, —

The moaning tide and the silent sun,
The wind and the stars and the Northern light,
Changing the watch by night.

And of all the travellers who questioned me,
Why I make my home in so quiet a land,

Not a soul could understand.

Till the day you came with love in your eyes,
And asked no more than the sun on the wall,
Yet understood it all.

And my house has been filled to overflow
With beauty and laughter and peace since then,
And joys of the world of men.


LXXXIII.

A woman sat by the hearth,
And a man looked out at the door.

"O lover, I hear a sound
As of approaching storm,
When the sea makes in from the north
With thunder and chafing and might,
And trundles the quaking ground."

"It is not the sea you hear.
The ice in the river is loosed;
You hear its grinding mills
Wearing the winter away,
And the grist of grief and cold
Shall soon be the meal of joy.
O heart of me, April is here!"

"O lover, I hear a sigh
As of the boding wind
In the murmurous black pines,
Or a stir as of beating wings
When the fleeing curlews fly."

"It is not the wind's great hum;
The bees in the willow blooms,
All golden-dusted now,
Sing in their chantry loft
As when earth the immortal was young,
Busy with ardour and joy.
O heart of mine, April is come!"

"O lover, my heart aches sore;
My hands would fondle your hair,
My cheek be laid to your cheek;

A strange new wild great word
Knocks at my heart's closed door."

"Who is not a learner now?
We endure, and seasons change,
And the heart grows great and strange
With the beauty of earth and time.
Our lives unfold and get free,
As the streams and the creatures do,
To range through the April now."

Like a gold spring-flower in his arms,
She stood by the open door.

LXXXIV.

The willows are all golden now,
And grief is past and olden now;
To the wild heart
There comes a start
Will help it and embolden now.

The birch tips are all slender now;
The April light is tender now;
And the soft skies
Are calm and wise
With vision of new splendour now.

The streets are full of gladness now, —
Forget their look of sadness now;
While up and down
The flowery town
Comes back the old spring madness now.

LXXXV.

O wonder of all wonders,
The winter time is done,
And to the low, bleak, bitter hills
Comes back the melting sun!

O wonder of all wonders,
The soft spring winds return,
And in the sweeping gusts of rain

The glowing tulips burn!

O wonder of all wonders,
That tenderness divine,
Bearing a woman's name, should knock
At this poor door of mine!


LXXXVI.

This is the time of the golden bough,
The April ardour, the mystic fire,
And the soft wind up from the South,
Lingering, rainy, and warm,
Dissolving sorrow and bidding new life aspire, —
New spirit take form, —
Through the waking green earth now.

This is the time of the golden tress,
The heaving heart and the shining glance,
And the little head that bows
Meekly to love at last.
Then two behold the flowery world in a trance
Through the spring's new vast
Of sunshine and tenderness.


LXXXVII.

When spring comes up the slope of the grey old sea,
Like a green galleon,
With joy in her wake, with light on her sails,
What will she bring to us, my Yvonne?

The long, sweet lisp and drench of the sweetness of rain,
The strong, glad youth of the sun,
And a touch of the madness that makes men wise
With the wisdom of lovers, my Yvonne.


LXXXVIII.

Now spring comes up the world, sweetheart,
What shall we find to do?
The hills grow purple in the rain,

The sea is gold and blue;

The door is open to the sun,
The window to the sky;
The odour of the cherry bough,
A freighted dream, goes by;

The spruces tell the southwest wind
Where the white windflowers are;
The brooks are babbling in the dusk
To one great yellow star;

In all the April-coloured land,
Where glints and murmurs stray,
There's not a being that draws breath
But will go mad to-day —

Go mad with piercing ecstasy,
Afoot, afloat, awing,
And wild with all the aching sweet
Delirium of spring.

Now April fills the world with love,
There's not a thing to do
But to be happy all night long,
Then glad the whole day through.


LXXXIX.

The rain on the roof is your laughter;
The wind in the eaves is your sigh;
The sun on the hills is your gladness
In Spring going by.

The sea to its uttermost morning,
Gold-fielded, unfrontiered and blue,
Is the light and the space and the splendour
My heart holds for you.


XC.

Sweetheart, sweetheart, delay no more,
Nor in this prosy street abide!
The fairy coach is at the door;

The fairy ship is on the tide.

For I have built of golden dreams,
And furnished with delight for thee,
And lit with wondrous starry beams,
A fairy place over sea.

Then, footman, up! Good horses, speed!
Then, lads, aboard and make all sail!
The wind is fair, the cable freed;
Now what can all the world avail?


XCI.

Out of the floor of the greenish sea
Flowers the scarlet moon,
Thrusting the tip of her budding lip
Through its watery sheath in the waiting June.

Out of the grey of forgotten things
My heart shall arise at full,
And illumine space to find your face
By a love-light quiet and wonderful.


XCII.

There's not a little boat, sweetheart,
That dances on the tide, —
There's not a nodding daisy-head
In all the meadows wide, —

In all the warm green orchards,
Where bright birds sing and stray,
There's not a whistling oriole
So glad as I this day.


XCIII.

She said, "In all the purple hills,
Where dance the lilies blue,
Where all day long the springing larks
Make fairy-tales come true,

"Where you can lie for hours and watch
The unfathomable sky,
There's not a breath of all the June
That's half so glad as I!"


XCIV.

I saw the ships come wing by wing
Up from the golden south with spring;
And great was the treasure they had in hold
Of food and raiment and gems and gold,
The loot and barter of many lands
Brought home by daring and hardy hands.

For love is the only seed that sows
The waste of the sea which no man knows.

My sailing thoughts came back to me
From faring over the great dream sea;
And every one was laden deep
With riches of memory to keep,
Laughter and joy and the smooth delight
Of the little friend and the starry night.

For love is the only seed that sows
The waste of the heart which no man knows.


XCV.

Up and up, they all come up
Out of the noon together,
The flowering sails on the slope of the sea
In the white spring weather.

In and in, they all draw in —
A streaming flock together —
From the lone and monstrous waste of sea
By a single tether.

Home, come home, they all make home
In a racing fleet together —
The little white wishes I sent to you
In the golden weather.

## XCVI.

I saw you in the gloaming, love,
When all the fleets were homing, love,
And under the large level moon the long grey
seas were combing, love.

I saw you tall and splendid, love,
And all my griefs were ended, love,
When on me, as I put to land, your seaward
eyes were bended, love.

The little boats were stranded, love,
And all their rich bales landed, love;
But all my wealth awaited me low-voiced and
gentle-handed, love.


## XCVII.

How unutterably lonely
Is the vast grey round of sea,
Till the yellow flower of heaven
Breaks and blossoms and gets free,
Lighting up the lilac spaces
With her golden density!
Hope of sailors and of lovers,
Swings the lantern of the sea.

Not the moon it was that lighted
One grey waste of heart I know,
Warmed with loving, touched with magic,
And made molten and aglow,
When your beauty flowered above it
From a twilight soft and slow.
Dearest face that still must beacon
Where your lover still must go!


## XCVIII.

Do you know the pull of the wind on the sea?
That is the thought of you over my heart,

The long soft breath of the soul drawing back to me,
From the desolate lone of outer space,
At dead of night when we are apart.

Do you know the sound of the surf on the shore,
At the lilac close of a soft spring day?
That is the fairy music I hear once more,
As I remember your last farewell,
In the blue still night when you are away.

And the wondrous round of the moon on the hill,
When blue dusk covers the rim of the sea?
More desired and strange and loved and lovelier still
Is the vision that comes with love in her eyes —
Your wonderful eyes — forever to me.


XCIX.

The fishers are sailing; the fleet is away;
The rowlocks are throbbing at break of day.

The cables are creaking; the sails are unfurled;
The red sun is over the rim of the world.

The first summer hour is white on the hill;
The sails in the harbour-mouth belly and fill, —

Each boat putting out with the breast of a gull
For the mighty great deep that shall rock them and lull.

There, there, they all pass out of sight one by one —
Gleam, dazzle, and sink in the path of the sun, —

The last tiny speck to melt out and be free
As a roseleaf of cloud on the rim of the sea.


C.

My love said, "What is the sea?"
I said, "The unmeasured sea
Is my heart, sweetheart,
That is stormy or still
With its great wild will,
Glorying, stainless and free,
Or sad with a sorrow beyond man's speech to impart,

But for ever calling to thee,
Heart of my heart."

My love said, "What is the tide?"
I said, "The unshackled tide
Is my love, sweetheart,
The draft and sweep
Of the restless deep,
Made clean as the stars and wide,
That forever must yearn to the land above and apart,
Till the day when she sinks to his side,
Heart of my heart."

My love said, "What is the land?"
I said, "The Summer land
Is thy face, sweetheart,
Dreamy and warm and glad,
In a benediction clad,
With sunshine sweetened and tanned;
And there is the set of the tide, the end and the start,
The sea's despair and demand,
Heart of my heart!"


CI.


The moonlight is a garden
Upon the mountainside,
Wherein your gleaming spirit
All lovely and grave-eyed,

Touched with the happy craving
That will not be denied,
Aforetime used to wander
Until it reached my side.

O wild white forest flower,
Rose-love and lily-pride,
And staunch of burning beauty
Against your lover's side!


CII.


The lily said to the rose,
"What will become of our pride,

When Yvonne comes down the path?"
And the crimson rose replied,

"Our beauty and pride must wane,
Yet we shall endure to stir
The pulse of lovers unborn
With metaphors of her."

CIII.

The white water-lilies, they sleep on the lake,
Till over the mountain the sun bids them wake.

At the rose-tinted touch of the long, level ray,
Each pure, perfect blossom unfolds to the day.

Each affluent petal outstretched and uncurled
To the glory and gladness and shine of the world.

O whiter land-lily, asleep in the dawn,
While yet the cool curtain of stars is half drawn,

And all the dark forest is mystic and still,
With the great yellow planet aglow on the hill,

Hark, somewhere among the grey beeches a thrush
Sends the first thrill of sound to requicken the hush!

With a flutter of eyelids, a sigh soft and deep,
An unfolding of rosy warm fingers from sleep,

For one perfect day more to love, gladden and roam,
Thy spirit comes back to its flowerlike home.

CIV.

What are the great stars white and blue,
Sparkling along the twilight there?
They are the dewy gems let fall,
When I loosed your hair.

What is the great pale, languorous moon
On the floor of the sea alone?
That is the yellow rose let fall,

When I loosed your zone.

What is that spreading light far over the sea,
In the thin cool dawn, in the wash of the summer air,
When the planets pale
And the soft winds fail
But Yvonne with her yellow hair?

What is that deep, dark shine in the heart of the sea,
The glory and glow and darkle and dim surprise,
Melting and clear
Beyond fathom of fear,
But Yvonne with her smoke-blue eyes?

What is that burning disk on the rim of the sea,
When autumn brushfires smoulder and birds go South,
When twilight fills
The imperial hills,
But Yvonne with her scarlet mouth?

Over the sea is a scarlet cloud,
And over the cloud the sun.
And over my heart is a shining hope,
And over that, Yvonne.

What lies across my lonely bed
Like tropic moonlight soft and pale?
What deeper gold is that outspread
Across my pillow like a vei?

What sudden fragrances are these
That voyage across the gloom to me,
With faint delirious ecstasies
From fairy gardens over sea?

What rustles in the curtained dusk
With the remembrance of a sigh,

As if a breath of wandering air
Should stir the poppies going by?

Lover of beauty, can it be
That from some far off foreign clime
The sumptuous night has brought to thee
The Rose of Beauty of all time?


CVIII.

Another day comes up,
Wears over, and goes down;
And it seems an age has passed
In a little seaboard town,

To one who must weary and wait
Till the sun comes round once more,
Before he may tap on the pane
And lift the latch of your door.


CIX.

Three things there be in the world, Yvonne;
And what do you guess they mean?
The stable land, the heaving sea,
And the tide that hangs between.

Three things there be in this life, Yvonne;
And what do you guess they mean?
Your sun-warm soul, my wind-swept soul,
And the current that draws between.


CX.

The first soft green of a Northern spring,
Lit by a golden sun:
That is the little frock you wore
When our love was begun,
In the house by the purple shore.

The gold-red flush of early fall,
And the tinge of sun on the sea:

That is the maiden vest you wore
When you came to my knee,
And the firelight danced on the floor.


CXI.

Now all the twigs and grasses
Are feathery with snow;
The land is white and level,
The brooks have ceased to flow.

No song is in the woodland,
There is no light of sun,
But bright and warm and tender
Is my sweetheart, Yvonne.

The lower hills are purple,
The farther peaks are lost;
There's nothing left alive now,
Except the bitter frost.

Yes, two there be that heed not
How cold the year may run:
The fire upon the hearthstone,
And my sweetheart, Yvonne.


CXII.

Our isle is a magic ship;
You can feel it swing and dip,
Running the long blue slopes
Of sliding sea,
With you and me
The only adventurers.

The sails of the snow are spread.
See how we forge ahead!
Good-by, old summers and sorrows!
O brave and dear
Whom never a fear
Of the breathless voyage deters!

CXIII.

The sails of the ship are white, love;
What are they?
The hauling clouds, you say.

The ropes are weather-worn, love;
What are they?
The strands of rain, you say.

The lights ashore are lit, love;
What are they?
The beacon stars, you say.

How shall we keep the course, love,
By night and day?
By a secret chart, you say.

But how shall we reckon true, love,
Without time of day?
By a tick of the heart, you say.

And how shall we know the land, love,
On that day?
You smile and will not say.


CXIV.

Look, where the northern streamers wave and fold,
Bluish and green and gold,

At the far corner of the quiet land,
Moved by an unseen hand!

Some one has drawn the curtains of the night,
And taken away the light.

It is so still I cannot hear a sound,
Except the mighty bound

Your little heart makes beating in your side,
And the first sob of tide,

When the sea turns from ebb far down the shore
To his old task once more.

O surging, stifling heart, have all your will,
In the blue night and still!

Love till the Hand folds up the firmament,
And the last stars are spent!


CXV.

I do not long for fame,
Nor triumph, nor trumpets of praise;
I only wish my name
To endure in the coming days,

When men say, musing at times,
With smiling speech and slow,
"He was a maker of rhymes
Yvonne loved long ago!"


CXVI.

I know how the great and golden sun
Will come up out of the sea,
Stride in to shore
And up to her door,
To touch her hand and her hair,
With so much more than a man can say,
Bidding Yvonne good day.

I know how the great and quiet moon
Will come up out of the sea,
And climb the hill
To her window-sill
And enter all silently,
And lie on her little cot so white,
Kissing Yvonne good night.

I know how the great and countless stars
Will come up out of the sea,
To keep their guard
By her still dooryard,
Lest the soul of Yvonne should stray
And be lost for ever there by the deep,
In the wonderful hills of sleep.

CXVII.

What will the Angel of the Morning say,
Relieving guard?
"Night, who hath passed thy way
To the Palace Yard?"
And Night will make reply,
"Only two springtime lovers sought
The King's reward."

Then will the Angel of the Morning say,
"What said the King?"
"The King said nought, but smiled
And took his ring
And gave it to the man,
And set him in his stead for one
Sweet day of spring."

Then will the Angel of the Morning say,
With grave regard,
"Pass, Night, and leave the gate
For once unbarred.
I serve the lover now;
He shall be free of all the earth
For his reward."


CXVIII.

Along the faint horizon
I watch the first soft green,
And for the first wild warble
Near to the ground I lean.

The flowers come up with colour,
The birds come back with song,
And from the earth are taken
Despondency and wrong.

Yet in the purple shadows,
And in the warm grey rain,
What hints of ancient sorrow
And unremembered pain!

O sob and flush of April,

That still must joy and sing!
What is the sad, wild meaning
Under the heart of Spring?


CXIX.

Once more the golden April;
Gold are the willow-trees,
And golden the soft murmur
Of the gold-belted bees.

All golden is the sunshine,
And golden are the flowers,
The golden-wing makes music
In the long, golden hours.

All dull gold are the marshes
And red gold are the dunes,
And gold the pollen dust is
Moting the quiet noons.

Even the sea's great sapphire
Is panelled with raw gold.
How else were spring unperished,
A thousand ages old?


CXX.

Now comes the golden sunlight
Up the glad earth once more,
And every forest dweller
Comes to his open door.

And now the quiet rain-wind
Comes from the soft grey sea,
To haunt thy April lover
With lonely pangs for thee!


CXXI.
In the blue mystery of the April woods,
Thy spirit now
Makes musical the rainbird's interludes,

And pink the peach-tree bough.

In the new birth of all things bright and fair,
'Tis only thou
Art very April, glory, light and air,
And joy and ardour now!


AFTERSONG

These are the joyous songs
The shy sea children sing,
When the moon goes down the west,
Soft as a pale moth wing;

When the gnat and the bumblebee
In the gauze of sleep are fast,
And a fairy summer dream
Is the only thing will last.

These are the ever-songs
The heart of the sea will sing,
When ash-coloured birds are building,
And lilac thickets ring;

When June is an open road
For every soul that stirs;
When scarlet voices summon,
And not a foot defers.

These are the twilight songs
Out of the simple North,
Where the marchers of the night
In silent troops go forth;

Where Alioth sails and sails
Forever round the pole,
And wonder brings no sad
Disquietude of soul.

And all their bodily beauty
Must flower a moment and die,
As the rain goes down the sea-rim,
The streamers up the sky;

Till time as a falling echo
Shall sift them over and o'er,

And the wind between the stars
Can tell their words no more.

Yet the lyric beat and cry
Which frets the poor frail things
Shall pass from joy to joy
Up through a thousand springs,

Teasing the sullen years
Out of monotony,
As reedbirds pour their rapture
By the unwintered sea.


## Bliss Carman - An Appreciation

How many Canadians—how many even among the few who seek to keep themselves informed of the
best in contemporary literature, who are ever on the alert for the new voices—realise, or even suspect,
that this Northern land of theirs has produced a poet of whom it may be affirmed with confidence and
assurance that he is of the great succession of English poets? Yet such—strange and unbelievable
though it may seem—is in very truth the case, that poet being (to give him his full name) William Bliss
Carman. Canada has full right to be proud of her poets, a small body though they are; but not only does
Mr. Carman stand high and clear above them all—his place (and time cannot but confirm and justify the
assertion) is among those men whose poetry is the shining glory of that great English literature which is
our common heritage.

If any should ask why, if what has been just said is so, there has been—as must be admitted—no general
recognition of the fact in the poet's home land, I would answer that there are various and plausible, if
not good, reasons for it.

First of all, the poet, as thousands more of our young men of ambition and confidence have done, went
early to the United States, and until recently, except for rare and brief visits to his old home down by the
sea, has never returned to Canada—though for all that, I am able to state, on his own authority, he is
still a Canadian citizen. Then all his books have had their original publication in the United States, and
while a few of them have subsequently carried the imprints of Canadian publishers, none of these can
be said ever to have made any special effort to push their sale. Another reason for the fact above
mentioned is that Mr. Carman has always scorned to advertise himself, while his work has never been
the subject of the log-rolling and booming which the work of many another poet has had—to his
ultimate loss. A further reason is that he follows a rule of his own in preparing his books for publication.
Most poets publish a volume of their work as soon as, through their industry and perseverance, they
have material enough on hand to make publication desirable in their eyes. Not so with Mr. Carman,
however, his rule being not to publish until he has done sufficient work of a certain general character or
key to make a volume. As a result, you cannot fully know or estimate his work by one book, or two
books, or even half a dozen; you must possess or be familiar with every one of the score and more
volumes which contain his output of poetry before you can realise how great and how many-sided is his
genius.

It is a common remark on the part of those who respond readily to the vigorous work of Kipling, or Masefield, even our own Service, that Bliss Carman's poetry has no relation to or concern with ordinary, everyday life. One would suppose that most persons who cared for poetry at all turned to it as a relief from or counter to the burdens and vexations of the daily round; but in any event, the remark referred to seems to me to indicate either the most casual acquaintance with Mr. Carman's work, or a complete misunderstanding and misapprehension of the meaning of it. I grant that you will find little or nothing in it all to remind you of the grim realities and vexing social problems of this modern existence of ours; but to say or to suggest that these things do not exist for Mr. Carman is to say or to suggest something which is the reverse of true. The truth is, he is aware of them as only one with the sensitive organism of a poet can be; but he does not feel that he has a call or mission to remedy them, and still less to sing of them. He therefore leaves the immediate problems of the day to those who choose, or are led, to occupy themselves therewith, and turns resolutely away to dwell upon those things which for him possess infinitely greater importance.

"What are they?" one who knows Mr. Carman only as, say, a lyrist of spring or as a singer of the delights of vagabondia probably will ask in some wonder. Well, the things which concern him above all, I would answer, are first, and naturally, the beauty and wonder of this world of ours, and next the mystery of the earthly pilgrimage of the human soul out of eternity and back into it again.

The poems in the present volume—which, by the way, can boast the high honor of being the very first regular Canadian edition of his work—will be evidence ample and conclusive to every reader, I am sure, of the place which

The perennial enchanted
Lovely world and all its lore

occupy in the heart and soul of Bliss Carman, as well as of the magical power with which he is able to convey the deep and unfailing satisfaction and delight which they possess for him. They, however, represent his latest period (he has had three well-defined periods), comprising selections from three of his last published volumes: The Rough Rider, Echoes from Vagabondia, and April Airs, together with a number of new poems, and do not show, except here and there and by hints and flashes, how great is his preoccupation with the problem of man's existence—

—the hidden import
Of man's eternal plight.

This is manifest most in certain of his earlier books, for in these he turns and returns to the greatest of all the problems of man almost constantly, probing, with consummate and almost unrivalled use of the art of expression, for the secret which surely, he clearly feels, lies hidden somewhere, to be discovered if one could but pierce deeply enough. Pick up Behind the Arras, and as you turn over page after page you cannot but observe how incessantly the poet's mind—like the minds of his two great masters, Browning and Whitman—works at this problem. In "Behind the Arras," the title poem; "In the Wings," "The Crimson House," "The Lodger," "Beyond the Gamut," "The Juggler"—yes, in every poem in the book—he takes up and handles the strange thing we know as, or call, life, turning it now this way, now that, in an effort to find out its meaning and purpose. He comes but little nearer success in this than do most of the rest of men, of course; but the magical and ever-fresh beauty of his expression, the haunting melody of his lines, the variety of his images and figures and the depth and range of his thought, put his searchings and ponderings in a class by themselves.

Lengthy quotation from Mr. Carman's books is not permitted here, and I must guide myself accordingly, though with reluctance, because I believe that in a study such as this the subject should be allowed to speak for himself as much as possible. In "Behind the Arras" the poet describes the passage from life to death as

A cadence dying down unto its source
In music's course,

and goes on to speak of death as

—the broken rhythm of thought and man,
The sweep and span
Of memory and hope
About the orbit where they still must grope
For wider scope,

To be through thousand springs restored, renewed,
With love imbrued,
With increments of will
Made strong, perceiving unattainment still
From each new skill.

Now follow some verses from "Behind the Gamut," to my mind the poet's greatest single achievement;

As fine sand spread on a disc of silver,
At some chord which bids the motes combine,
Heeding the hidden and reverberant impulse,
Shifts and dances into curve and line,

The round earth, too, haply, like a dust-mote,
Was set whirling her assigned sure way,
Round this little orb of her ecliptic
To some harmony she must obey.

And what of man?

Linked to all his half-accomplished fellows,
Through unfrontiered provinces to range—
Man is but the morning dream of nature,
Roused to some wild cadence weird and strange.

Here, now, are some verses from "Pulvis et Umbra," which is to be found in Mr. Carman's first book, Low Tide on Grand Pré, and in which the poet addresses a moth which a storm has blown into his window:

For man walks the world with mourning
Down to death and leaves no trace,
With the dust upon his forehead,

And the shadow on his face.

Pillared dust and fleeing shadow
As the roadside wind goes by,
And the fourscore years that vanish
In the twinkling of an eye.

"Pillared dust and fleeing shadow." Where in all our English literature will one find the life history of man summed up more briefly and, at the same time, more beautifully, than in that wonderful line? Now follows a companion verse to those just quoted, taken from "Lord of My Heart's Elation," which stands in the forefront of From the Green Book of the Bards. It may be remarked here that while the poet recurs again and again to some favorite thought or idea, it is never in the same words. His expression is always new and fresh, showing how deep and true is his inspiration. Again it is man who is pictured:

A fleet and shadowy column
Of dust and mountain rain,
To walk the earth a moment
And be dissolved again.

But while Mr. Carman's speculations upon life's meaning and the mystery of the future cannot but appeal to the thoughtful-minded, it is as an interpreter of nature that he makes his widest appeal. Bliss Carman, I must say here, and emphatically, is no mere landscape-painter; he never, or scarcely ever, paints a picture of nature for its own sake. He goes beyond the outward aspect of things and interprets or translates for us with less keen senses as only a poet whose feeling for nature is of the deepest and profoundest, who has gone to her whole-heartedly and been taken close to her warm bosom, can do. Is this not evident from these verses from "The Great Return"—originally called "The Pagan's Prayer," and for some inscrutable reason to be found only in the limited Collected Poems, issued in two stately volumes in 1905.

When I have lifted up my heart to thee,
Thou hast ever hearkened and drawn near,
And bowed thy shining face close over me,
Till I could hear thee as the hill-flowers hear.

When I have cried to thee in lonely need,
Being but a child of thine bereft and wrung,
Then all the rivers in the hills gave heed;
And the great hill-winds in thy holy tongue—

That ancient incommunicable speech—
The April stars and autumn sunsets know—
Soothed me and calmed with solace beyond reach
Of human ken, mysterious and low.

Who can read or listen to those moving lines without feeling that Mr. Carman is in very truth a poet of nature—nay, Nature's own poet? But how could he be other when, in "The Breath of the Reed" (From the Green Book of the Bards), he makes the appeal?

Make me thy priest, O Mother,
And prophet of thy mood,
With all the forest wonder
Enraptured and imbued.

As becomes such a poet, and particularly a poet whose birth-month is April, Mr. Carman sings much of the early spring. Again and again he takes up his woodland pipe, and lo! Pan himself and all his train troop joyously before us. Yet the singer's notes for all his singing never become wearied or strident; his airs are ever new and fresh; his latest songs are no less spontaneous and winning than were his first, written how many years ago, while at the same time they have gained in beauty and melody. What heart will not stir to the vibrant music of his immortal "Spring Song," which was originally published in the first Songs from Vagabondia, and the opening verses of which follow?

Make me over, mother April,
When the sap begins to stir!
When thy flowery hand delivers
All the mountain-prisoned rivers,
And thy great heart beats and quivers
To revive the days that were,
Make me over, mother April,
When the sap begins to stir!

Take my dust and all my dreaming,
Count my heart-beats one by one,
Send them where the winters perish;
Then some golden noon recherish
And restore them in the sun,
Flower and scent and dust and dreaming,
With their heart-beats every one!

That poem is sufficient in itself to prove that Bliss Carman has full right and title to be called Spring's own lyrist, though it may be remarked here that not all his spring poems are so unfeignedly joyous. Many of them indeed, have a touch, or more than a touch, of wistfulness, for the poet knows well that sorrow lurks under all joy, deep and well hidden though it may be.

Mr. Carman sings equally finely, though perhaps not so frequently, of summer and the other seasons; but as he has other claims upon our attention, I shall forbear to labor the fact, particularly as the following collection demonstrates it sufficiently. One of those other claims is as a writer of sea poetry. Few poets, it may be said, have pictured the majesty and the mystery, the beauty and the terror of the sea, better than he. His Ballads of Lost Haven is a veritable treasure-house for those whose spirits find kinship in wide expanses of moving waters. One of the best known poems in this volume is "The Gravedigger," which opens thus:

Oh, the shambling sea is a sexton old,
And well his work is done.
With an equal grave for lord and knave,
He buries them every one.

Then hoy and rip, with a rolling hip,
He makes for the nearest shore;
And God, who sent him a thousand ship,
Will send him a thousand more;
But some he'll save for a bleaching grave,
And shoulder them in to shore—
Shoulder them in, shoulder them in,
Shoulder them in to shore.

In "The City of the Sea" (Last Songs from Vagabondia) Mr. Carman speaks of the seabells sounding

The eternal cadence of sea sorrow
For Man's lot and immemorial wrong—
The lost strains that haunt the human dwelling
With the ghost of song.

Elsewhere he speaks of

The great sea, mystic and musical.

And here from another poem is a striking picture:

... the old sea
Seems to whimper and deplore
Mourning like a childless crone
With her sorrow left alone—
The eternal human cry
To the heedless passer-by.

I have said above that Mr. Carman has had three distinct periods, and intimated that the poems in the following collection are of his third period. The first period may be said to be represented by the Low Tide and Behind the Arras volumes, while the second is displayed in the three volumes of Songs from Vagabondia, which he published in association with his friend Richard Hovey. Bliss Carman was from the first too original and individual a poet to be directly influenced by anyone else; but there can be no doubt that his friendship with Hovey helped to turn him from over-preoccupation with mysteries which, for all their greatness, are not for man to solve, to an intenser realisation of the beauty and loveliness of the world about him and of the joys of human fellowship. The result is seen in such poems as "Spring Song," quoted in part above, and his perhaps equally well-known "The Joys of the Road," which appeared in the same volume with that poem, and a few verses from which follow:

Now the joys of the road are chiefly these:
A crimson touch on the hardwood trees;

A vagrant's morning wide and blue,
In early fall, when the wind walks, too;

A shadowy highway cool and brown,
Alluring up and enticing down

From rippled waters and dappled swamp,
From purple glory to scarlet pomp;

The outward eye, the quiet will,
And the striding heart from hill to hill.

Some of the finest of arman's work is contained in his elegiac or memorial poems, in which he commemorates Keats, Shelley, William Blake, Lincoln, Stevenson, and other men for whom he has a kindred feeling, and also friends whom he has loved and lost. Listen to these moving lines from "Non Omnis Moriar," written in memory of Gleeson White, and to be found in Last Songs from Vagabondia:

There is a part of me that knows,
Beneath incertitude and fear,
I shall not perish when I pass
Beyond mortality's frontier;

But greatly having joyed and grieved,
Greatly content, shall hear the sigh
Of the strange wind across the lone
Bright lands of taciturnity.

In patience therefore I await
My friend's unchanged benign regard,—
Some April when I too shall be
Spilt water from a broken shard.

In "The White Gull," written for the centenary of the birth of Shelley in 1892, and included in By the Aurelian Wall, he thus apostrophizes that clear and shining spirit:

O captain of the rebel host,
Lead forth and far!
Thy toiling troopers of the night
Press on the unavailing fight;
The sombre field is not yet lost,
With thee for star.

Thy lips have set the hail and haste
Of clarions free
To bugle down the wintry verge
Of time forever, where the surge
Thunders and trembles on a waste
And open sea.

In "A Seamark," a threnody for Robert Louis Stevenson, which appears in the same volume, the poet hails "R.L.S." (of whose tribe he may be said to be truly one) as

The master of the roving kind,

and goes on:

O all you hearts about the world
In whom the truant gypsy blood,
Under the frost of this pale time,
Sleeps like the daring sap and flood
That dreams of April and reprieve!
You whom the haunted vision drives,
Incredulous of home and ease.
Perfection's lovers all your lives!

You whom the wander-spirit loves
To lead by some forgotten clue
Forever vanishing beyond
Horizon brinks forever new;
Our restless loved adventurer,
On secret orders come to him,
Has slipped his cable, cleared the reef,
And melted on the white sea-rim.

"Perfection's lovers all your lives." Of these, it may be said without qualification, is Bliss Carman himself.

No summary of Mr. Carman's work, however cursory, would be worthy of the name if it omitted mention of his ventures in the realm of Greek myth. From the Book of Myths is made up of work of that sort, every poem in it being full of the beauty of phrase and melody of which Mr. Carman alone has the secret. The finest poems in the book, barring the opening one, "Overlord," are "Daphne," "The Dead Faun," "Hylas," and "At Phædra's Tomb," but I can do no more here than name them, for extracts would fail to reveal their full beauty. And beauty, after all is said, is the first and last thing with Mr. Carman. As he says himself somewhere:

The joy of the hand that hews for beauty
Is the dearest solace under the sun.

And again

The eternal slaves of beauty
Are the masters of the world.

A slave—a happy, willing slave—to beauty is the poet himself, and the world can never repay him for the message of beauty which he has brought it.

Kindred to From the Book of Myths, but much more important, is Sappho: One Hundred Lyrics, one of the most successful of the numerous attempts which have been made to recapture the poems by that high priestess of song which remain to us only in fragments. Mr. Carman, as Charles G. D. Roberts points out in an introduction to the volume, has made no attempt here at translation or paraphrasing; his venture has been "the most perilous and most alluring in the whole field of poetry"—that of imaginative and, at the same time, interpretive construction. Brief quotation again would fail to convey an adequate idea of the exquisiteness of the work, and all I can do, therefore, is to urge all lovers of real poetry to possess themselves of Sappho: One Hundred Lyrics, for it is literally a storehouse of lyric beauty.

I must not fail here to speak of From the Book of Valentines, which contains some lovely things, notably "At the Great Release." This is not only one of the finest of all Mr. Carman's poems, but it is also one of the finest poems of our time. It is a love poem, and no one possessing any real feeling for poetry can read it without experiencing that strange thrill of the spirit which only the highest form of poetry can communicate. "Morning and Evening," "In an Iris Meadow," and "A letter from Lesbos" must be also mentioned. In the last named poem, Sappho is represented as writing to Gorgo, and expresses herself in these moving words:

If the high gods in that triumphant time
Have calendared no day for thee to come
Light-hearted to this doorway as of old,
Unmoved I shall behold their pomps go by—
The painted seasons in their pageantry,
The silvery progressions of the moon,
And all their infinite ardors unsubdued,
Pass with the wind replenishing the earth

Incredulous forever I must live
And, once thy lover, without joy behold,
The gradual uncounted years go by,
Sharing the bitterness of all things made.

Mention must be now made of Songs of the Sea Children, which can be described only as a collection of the sweetest and tenderest love lyrics written in our time—

—the lyric songs
The earthborn children sing,
When wild-wood laughter throngs
The shy bird-throats of spring;
When there's not a joy of the heart
But flies like a flag unfurled,
And the swelling buds bring back
The April of the world.

So perfect and complete are these lyrics that it would be almost sacrilege to quote any of them unless entire. Listen however, to these verses:

The day is lost without thee,
The night has not a star.
Thy going is an empty room
Whose door is left ajar.

Depart: it is the footfall
Of twilight on the hills.

Return: and every rood of ground
Breaks into daffodils.

There are those who will have it that Bliss Carman has been away from Canada so long that he has ceased to be, in a real sense, a Canadian. Such assume rather than know, for a very little study of his work would show them that it is shot through and through with the poet's feeling for the land of his birth. Memories of his childhood and youthful years down by the sea are still fresh in Mr. Carman's mind, and inspire him again and again in his writing. "A Remembrance," at the beginning of the present collection, may be pointed to as a striking instance of this, but proof positive is the volume, Songs from a Northern Garden, for it could have been written only by a Canadian, born and bred, one whose heart and soul thrill to the thought of Canada. I would single out from this volume for special mention as being "Canadian" in the fullest sense "In a Grand Pré Garden," "The Keeper's Silence," "At Home and Abroad," "Killoleet," and "Above the Gaspereau," but have no space to quote from them.

But Mr. Carman is not only a Canadian, he is also a Briton; and evidence of this is his Ode on the Coronation, written on the occasion of the crowning of King Edward VII in 1902. This poem—the very existence of which is hardly known among us—ought to be put in the hands of every child and youth who speaks the English tongue, for no other, I dare maintain—nothing by Kipling, or Newbolt, or any other of our so-called "Imperial singers"—expresses more truly and more movingly the deep feeling of love and reverence which the very thought of England evokes in every son of hers, even though it may never have been his to see her white cliffs rise or to tread her storied ground:

O England, little mother by the sleepless Northern tide,
Having bred so many nations to devotion, trust, and pride,
Very tenderly we turn
With welling hearts that yearn
Still to love you and defend you,—let the sons of men discern
Wherein your right and title, might and majesty, reside.

In concluding this, I greatly fear, lamentably inadequate study, I come to the collection which follows, and which, as intimated above, represents the work of Mr. Carman's latest period. I must say at once that, while I yield to no one in admiration for Low Tide and the other books of that period, or for the work of the second period, as represented by the Songs from Vagabondia volumes, I have no hesitation in declaring that I regard the poet's work of the past few years with even higher admiration. It may not possess the force and vigor of the work which preceded it; but anything seemingly missing in that respect is more than made up for me by increased beauty and clarity of expression. The mysticism—verging, or more than verging, at times on symbolism—which marked his earlier poems, and which hung, as it were, as a veil between them and the reader, has gone, and the poet's thought or theme now lies clearly before us as in a mirror. What—to take a verse from the following pages at random—could be more pellucid, more crystal clear in expression—what indeed, could come closer to that achieving of the impossible at which every real poet must aim—than this from "In Gold Lacquer".

Gold are the great trees overhead,
And gold the leaf-strewn grass,
As though a cloth of gold were spread
To let a seraph pass.
And where the pageant should go by,
Meadow and wood and stream,

The world is all of lacquered gold,
Expectant as a dream.

The poet, happily, has fully recovered from the serious illness which laid him low some two years ago, and which for a time caused his friends and admirers the gravest concern, and so we may look forward hopefully to seeing further volumes of verse come from the press to make certain his name and fame. But if, for any reason, this should not be—which the gods forfend!—Later Poems, I dare affirm, must and will be regarded as the fine flower and crowning achievement of the genius and art of Bliss Carman.

*R. H. HATHAWAY.*
*Toronto, 1921.*

## Bliss Carman – A Short Biography

William Bliss Carman was born in Fredericton, in New Brunswick on April 15th 1861. 'Bliss' was his mother's maiden name. She was descended from Daniel Bliss of Concord, Massachusetts, who was the great-grandfather to Ralph Waldo Emerson.

Carman was educated at Fredericton Collegiate School. Here, under the influence of the headmaster George Robert Parkin, he gained an appreciation of classical literature and was introduced to the poetry of many of the Pre-Raphaelites especially Dante Gabriel Rossetti and Algernon Charles Swinburne.

From here he graduated to the University of New Brunswick, obtaining his B.A. there in 1881. As is common with so many writers his first published piece was for the University magazine and for Carman that was in 1879.

England now beckoned and he spent a year at Oxford and then the University of Edinburgh (1882–1883). He returned home to Canada to work on his M.A. which he obtained from the University of New Brunswick in 1884.

Tragically his father died in January, 1885, followed by his mother in February of the following year. Carman now enrolled in Harvard University for a year. There he met and was part of a literary circle that included the American poet Richard Hovey, who would become his close friend, and later collaborator, on the successful Vagabondia poetry series. Carman and Hovey were members of the "Visionists" circle along with Herbert Copeland and F. Holland Day, who would later form the Boston publishing firm Copeland & Day and, in turn, launch Vagabondia.

After Harvard Carman briefly returned to Canada, but was back in Boston by February of 1890 saying "Boston is one of the few places where my critical education and tastes could be of any use to me in earning money. New York and London are about the only other places." However, he was unable to find work in Boston but was more successful in New York becoming the literary editor of the semi-religious New York Independent. There he helped Canadian poets get published and introduced them to a wider readership than they could receive in Canada.

However, Carman and work as an editor were not destined for a long career together and he was dismissed in 1892. There followed short stays with Current Literature, Cosmopolitan, The Chap-Book, and The Atlantic Monthly. Whilst these appointments provided the basis for a career and an income he was not suited to their demands. From 1895 he would only work as a contributor to magazines and newspapers whilst he worked on his volumes of poetry.

Carman first published a book of poetry in 1893 with Low Tide on Grand Pré. He had written the title poem in the summer of 1886 and it had (whilst he was still at Harvard) been published in the spring of 1887 by Atlantic Monthly. Despite its critical acceptance there was no Canadian company prepared to publish the volume. When an American company did so it went bankrupt. Life was becoming difficult for the young poet.

The following year was decidedly better. His partnership with Richard Hovey had given birth to Songs of Vagabondia and it was published by their friends at Copeland & Day. It was an immediate success. The young men were delighted at such a reception. It quickly sold out and was re-printed a number of times. Although these re-prints were small (usually 500-1000 copies) they were frequent.

On the back of this success they would write a further three volumes, which in their turn were almost as successful. They quickly became the center of a cult following, especially among students who empathized with the poetry's anti-materialistic themes, its celebration of personal freedom, and its glorification of comradeship."

The success of Songs of Vagabondia prompted the Boston firm, Stone & Kimball, to reissue Low Tide on Grand Pré and to hire Carman as the editor of its literary journal, The Chapbook. This ceased after a year when the company relocated and Carman expressed his desire to remain in Boston.

In 1885 Carman brought out Behind the Arras, a somewhat more serious and philosophical work centered on the premise of a long meditation using the speaker's house and its many rooms as a symbol of life and the choices to be made. However, the idea and its execution did not quite meld.

Signficantly, in 1896, Carman met Mrs Mary Perry King, who rapidly became patron, adviser and sometime lover. She put money in his pocket, and food in his mouth and, when he struck bottom, often repaired his confidence as well as helping to sell the work. She also later became his writing collaborator on two verse dramas.

Mitchell Kennerley, Carman's roommate wrote that, "On the rare occasions they had intimate relations they always advised me of by leaving a bunch of violets — Mary favorite flower — on the pillow of my bed." If her husband, Dr. King, knew of this arrangement he seems not to have objected. He was a great supporter of Carman's career and seemingly his wife's complicated involvement with that.

In 1897 Carman published Ballad of Lost Haven, a collection of poetry about the sea. Its notable poems include the macabre sea shanty, The Gravedigger. The following year, 1898, came By the Aurelian Wall, the title poem itself was an elegy to John Keats and the book a collection of formal elegies.

In 1899 his publisher, Lamson, Wolffe was taken over by the Boston firm of Small, Maynard & Co., who had also acquired the rights to Low Tide on Grand Pré. The copyrights to of his books were now held by one publisher and, in lieu of earnings, Carman took what would ultimately be a disastrous financial stake in the company.

As the century turned Carman was hard at work on what would eventually be a five-volume set of poetry; "Pans Pipes". Pan, the goat-god, was traditionally associated with poetry and the coming together of the earthly and the divine. The five volumes were all published between 1902 – 1905.

The inspiration for this came from Mary who had persuaded Carman to write in both prose and poetry about the ideas of 'unitrinianism.' This drew on the theories of François-Alexandre-Nicolas-Chéri Delsarte and was defined as a strategy of mind-body-spirit harmonization aimed at undoing the physical, psychological, and spiritual damage caused by urban modernity. The definition may be rather woolly but for Carman it resulted in some very fine work across the five-volume series. This shared belief between Mary and Carman created a further bond but did isolate him from his circle of friends.

The excellence of a number of these poems did much to install Carman as the most noted of Canadian Poets and eventually their own Poet Laureate. Among the most often quoted and printed are "The Dead Faun" (from Volume I), "Lord of My Heart's Elation" (Volume II) and many of the erotic poems from Volume III.

In the middle of publication in 1903, Small, Maynard failed and with it went all the assets Carman had tied up in the company.

Carman immediately signed with another Boston publisher, L.C. Page, who would publish seven new books of Carman poetry in this hectic period up to 1905. They released a further three books based on Carman's Transcript columns, and a prose work on Unitrinianism, The Making of Personality, that he'd written with Mary King.

Carman now felt secure enough to pursue his 'dream project,' namely a deluxe edition of his collected poetry to 1903. Page acquired the distribution rights on the condition that the book be sold privately, by subscription. Unfortunately, the demand wasn't there and it failed. Carman was deeply disappointed and lost faith in Page. However, their grip on his copyrights was absolute and sadly no further collected editions were to be published during his lifetime.

By 1904 his income was restricted and the offer to be editor-in-chief of the 10-volume project, The World's Best Poetry, was eagerly accepted.

For Carman perhaps his best years as a poet were now behind him. From 1908 he lived near the Kings' New Canaan, Connecticut, estate, that he named "Sunshine", or in the summer in a cabin in the Catskills, which he called "Moonshine."

With Literary tastes now moving away from what he could provide his income further dwindled and his health started to deteriorate.

In 1912 Carman published the final work in the Vagabondia series. Richard Hovey had died in 1900 and so this last work was purely his. It has a distinct elegiac tone as if remembering the past works themselves.

Although Carman was not politically active he did campaign during the World War One, as a member of the Vigilantes, who supported the American entry into the titanic struggle on the Allied side.

By 1920, Carman was impoverished and recovering from a near-fatal attack of tuberculosis. He returned to Canada and began to undertake a series of publicly successful and somewhat lucrative reading tours, saying "there is nothing worth talking of in book sales compared with reading. Breathless attention, crowded halls, and a strange, profound enthusiasm such as I never guessed could be,' he reported to a friend. 'And good thrifty money too. Think of it! An entirely new life for me, and I am the most surprised person in Canada.'"

On October 28th, 1921 Carman was honored at a dinner held by the newly-formed Canadian Authors' Association, at the Ritz Carlton Hotel in Montreal, where he was crowned Canada's Poet Laureate with a wreath of maple leaves.

Carman is placed among the Confederation Poets, a group that included his cousin, Charles G.D. Roberts, Archibald Lampman, and Duncan Campbell Scott. Carman was perhaps the best and is credited with the widest recognition. However, whilst the others carefully supplemented their income with writing novels and works for the magazines, or even other careers, Carman only wrote poetry together with a small amount of writing on literary ideas, philosophy, and aesthetics.

He continued his reading tours, and by 1925 had finally secured a new Canadian publisher; McClelland & Stewart (Toronto), who issued a collection of selected earlier verse and would now became his main publisher. Although they benefited from Carman's increased popularity and his revered position in Canadian literature, his former publisher L.C. Page would not relinquish its copyrights to his earlier works.

In his last years, Carman was a member of the Halifax literary and social set, The Song Fishermen and in 1927 he edited The Oxford Book of American Verse.

William Bliss Carman died of a brain hemorrhage, at the age of 68, in New Canaan on the 8th June, 1929. He was cremated in New Canaan and his ashes interred at Forest Hill Cemetery, Fredericton, with a national memorial service held at the Anglican cathedral there.

It was only a quarter of a century later, on May 13th, 1954, that a scarlet maple tree was planted at his graveside, to honour his request in the 1892 poem "The Grave-Tree":

Let me have a scarlet maple
For the grave-tree at my head,
With the quiet sun behind it,
In the years when I am dead.


Bliss Carman – A Concise Bibliography

Poetry Collections
Low Tide on Grand Pre: A Book of Lyrics (1893)
Songs from Vagabondia (1894)
A Seamark: A Threnody for Robert Louis Stevenson (1895)
Behind the Arras: A Book of the Unseen (1895)
More Songs from Vagabondia (1896)

Ballads of Lost Haven: A Book of the Sea (1897)
By the Aurelian Wall: And Other Elegies (1898)
A Winter Holiday (1899)
Last Songs from Vagabondia (1901)
Ballads and Lyrics (1902)
Ode on the Coronation of King Edward (1902)
Pipes of Pan: From the Book of Myths (1902)
Pipes of Pan: From the Green Book of the Bards (1903)
Pipes of Pan: Songs of the Sea Children (1904)
Pipes of Pan: Songs from a Northern Garden (1904)
Pipes of Pan: From the Book of Valentines (1905)
Sappho: One Hundred Lyrics (1904)
Poems (1905)
The Rough Rider: And Other Poems (1909)
A Painter's Holiday, and Other Poems (1911)
Echoes from Vagabondia (1912)
April Airs: A Book of New England Lyrics (1916)
The Man of The Marne: And Other Poems (1918)
The Vengeance of Noel Brassard: A Tale of the Acadian Expulsion (1919)
Far Horizons (1925)
Later Poems (1926)
Sanctuary: Sunshine House Sonnets (1929)
Wild Garden (1929)
Bliss Carman's Poems (1931)


Drama
Bliss Carman & Mary Perry King. Daughters of Dawn: A Lyrical Pageant of a Series of Historical Scenes for Presentation with Music and Dancing (1913)
Bliss Carman & Mary Perry King. Earth Deities: And Other Rhythmic Masques (1914)


Prose Collections
The Kinship of Nature (1904)
The Poetry of Life (1905)
The Friendship of Art (1908)
The Making of Personality (1908)
Talks on Poetry and Life; Being a Series of Five Lectures Delivered Before the University of Toronto, December 1925 (Speech). transcribed by Blanche Hume. 1926.
Bliss Carman's Scrap-Book: A Table of Contents (Pierce, Lorne, editor) (1931)


Editor
The World's Best Poetry (10 volumes) (1904)
The Oxford Book of American Verse (U.S. editor) (1927)
Carman, Bliss; Pierce, Lorne, editors (1935). Our Canadian Literature: Representative Verse, English and French.

www.ingramcontent.com/pod-product-compliance
Lightning Source LLC
Chambersburg PA
CBHW060145050426
42448CB00010B/2309